Seeing Both Sides

Homework,
Yes or No

Reese Everett

Rourke
EDUCATIONAL MEDIA

rourkeeducationalmedia.com

*Scan for Related Titles
and Teacher Resources*

Before Reading:

Building Academic Vocabulary and Background Knowledge

Before reading a book, it is important to tap into what your child or students already know about the topic. This will help them develop their vocabulary, increase their reading comprehension, and make connections across the curriculum.

1. *Look at the cover of the book. What will this book be about?*
2. *What do you already know about the topic?*
3. *Let's study the Table of Contents. What will you learn about in the book's chapters?*
4. *What would you like to learn about this topic? Do you think you might learn about it from this book? Why or why not?*
5. *Use a reading journal to write about your knowledge of this topic. Record what you already know about the topic and what you hope to learn about the topic.*
6. *Read the book.*
7. *In your reading journal, record what you learned about the topic and your response to the book.*
8. *After reading the book complete the activities below.*

Content Area Vocabulary
Read the list. What do these words mean?

allotted
complex
effective
element
isolated
mischief
position
proponents
resentment
sacrifice

After Reading:

Comprehension and Extension Activity

After reading the book, work on the following questions with your child or students in order to check their level of reading comprehension and content mastery.

1. *What is an opinion? (Summarize)*
2. *Explain why two people might have the same opinion for different reasons. (Infer)*
3. *What does homework allow you to do that can't be done in the classroom? (Asking questions)*
4. *How much time do you spend doing homework each day? (Text to self connection)*
5. *What are people who think critically more likely to do? (Asking questions)*

Extension Activity

You be the teacher! Create a homework assignment that requires students to think about a topic from different points of view. What sources should they use to find information? How should they present the information they discover?

Table of Contents

Taking Sides

What is your opinion about homework? Do your classmates agree with you? What about your parents and teachers?

An opinion is someone's belief based on experience and the information available to them. People can have different opinions about an issue.

Someone is more likely to understand your opinion if you talk about it using facts and details, even if they don't agree with you.

Homework is an issue many people have strong opinions about. Let's look at arguments on both sides of the issue.

Homework? Yes, Please!

Teachers have a lot of material to cover during each school day. The **allotted** time for a lesson may only allow students to explore the basics.

With so much to learn, there simply isn't enough time to do it all in the classroom. Homework is necessary because it extends learning beyond the school day.

Reality ✓

Students in countries such as Japan, Germany, and France are required to work on challenging subject matter at least twice as long as students in the United States.

In addition to giving you more time to learn, homework lets you practice learning independently.

Without a teacher and classmates at home to help, you only have yourself to rely on.

Homework gives you an opportunity to discover things that may not be covered in the classroom. It also lets you practice using resources such as the public library and the Internet to study a topic.

Learning how to study is just as important as studying a particular topic. Homework teaches you both the material and how to learn on your own.

Since every student learns differently, homework puts you in charge.

Homework develops positive study skills. Because your studies become more **complex**, or difficult, each year, you should begin developing good study habits at an early age.

Reality ✓

Researchers say homework teaches students the importance of responsibility, time management, good study habits, and staying with a task until it is completed.

Homework gives students time to think more creatively and critically. A book report may involve reading the book, researching the author, designing a poster, and writing an essay. Completing each **element** gives you a valuable experience you wouldn't have time to do if all of your work had to be done in school.

Homework can help students develop important skills, which include a variety of abilities that help people make decisions and consider multiple solutions to problems. Taking plenty of time to read, think, and discover outside of the classroom can improve students' ability to think critically.

Reality ✔

Studies have shown that critical thinking skills make people more likely to be involved citizens.

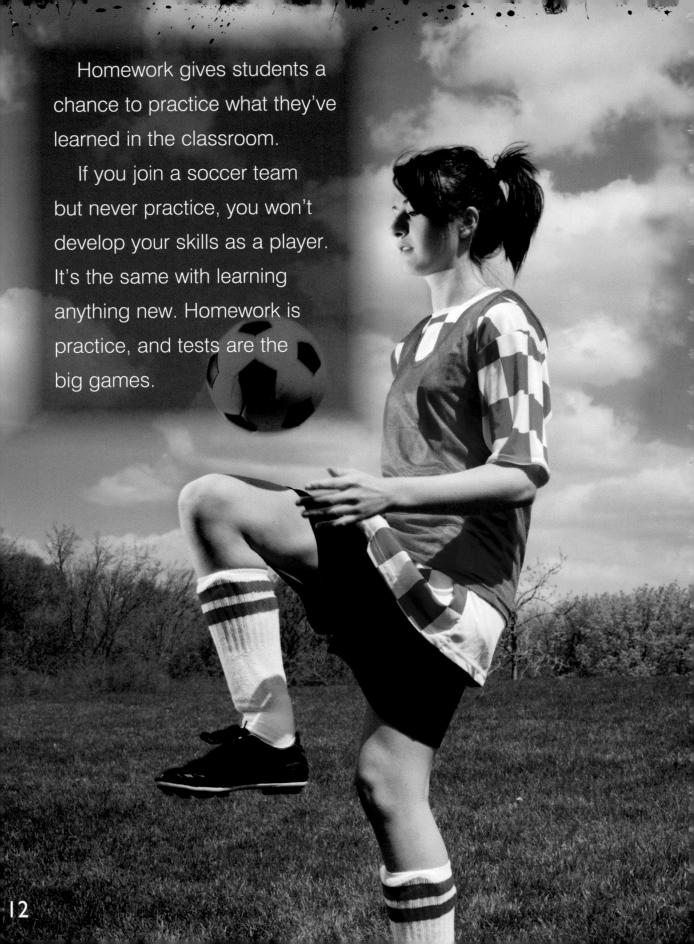

Homework gives students a chance to practice what they've learned in the classroom.

If you join a soccer team but never practice, you won't develop your skills as a player. It's the same with learning anything new. Homework is practice, and tests are the big games.

Homework assignments can show students what they do–and don't–understand. If you perform poorly on a homework assignment, you know you need to study more before a test. A bad homework grade also lets your teacher know you need more help in the classroom.

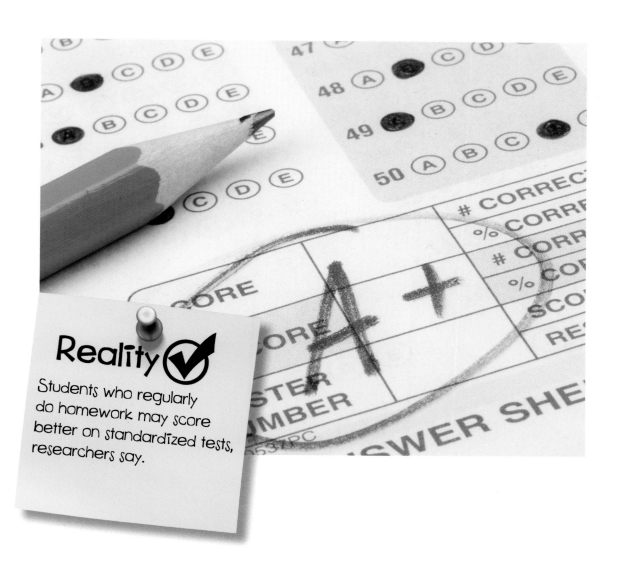

Reality ✓

Students who regularly do homework may score better on standardized tests, researchers say.

Homework helps you learn to be responsible. If you have an assignment due the next day, you have to make that a priority. Planning your time wisely is an important lesson homework provides.

Monday after school schedule

1. Homework
2. Dinner
3. Finish homework assignment due tomorrow!
4. Get a good night's sleep!

Some students think it is unfair to have assignments during summer vacation. But what happens to your brain when you take two months off from learning?

Experts say all young people experience learning losses if they don't participate in educational activities during the summer.

Reality ✓

Most students lose about two months of grade level equivalency in mathematical skills over the summer months.

If you have homework after school and during the summer, you don't have much time to get bored. Boredom can lead to trouble. If you have nothing to do after school, it may be tempting to bug your sibling or get into **mischief**.

In addition, homework assignments show your parents what you're learning.

Reality ✓

Research shows that homework assignments involving student-parent interactions are more likely to be turned in than non-interactive assignments.

Homework? No Way!

There are many reasons teachers should not assign homework.

Students spend most of their day in a classroom, so their free time should be spent doing what they want. Kids need time to relax. They need time to participate in activities they enjoy, whether it's sports, music, or just riding their bikes all over the neighborhood.

Homework can prevent students from discovering what they really enjoy doing. There is no time for them to read about interesting topics, or think about their own ideas, because they are too busy trying to keep up with their homework. By the time they are finished, they are too tired to do anything else.

Reality ✓

Some researchers say students that have too much homework do not have a healthy life balance.

Students spend most of their time at home studying and completing assignments. This prevents them from spending time with family and friends, which can make them feel **isolated**.

Parents want to spend time with their kids, but homework can interfere.

Homework causes stress for families when the student doesn't want to work on an assignment. Parents may feel pressure to force the child to do the homework, which can cause arguments, tears, and frustration.

Homework forces parents to **sacrifice** family time for homework time. Some homework is given because schools have decided that children must do some type of work every night.

Students often say they do not get enough sleep because they have too much homework. They stay up late to finish it all rather than going to bed at a reasonable time.

When you are not getting enough sleep because you stay up late to do homework, it may cause you to be less focused when you are in school.

Reality ✓

Sleep deprivation can cause a variety of health problems for kids and adults, such as heart disease, depression, and obesity.

Some people say that homework teaches responsibility. But students who have homework every night have less time to contribute to their responsibilities at home.

Life experiences are important. Students can learn about money management, personal responsibility, **effective** communication, and time management by working at home for an allowance or at a part-time job. What kind of homework can teach you all of that?

Reality ✓

Participating in extra-curricular activities, such as sports, music, art, or clubs, benefits students more than homework.

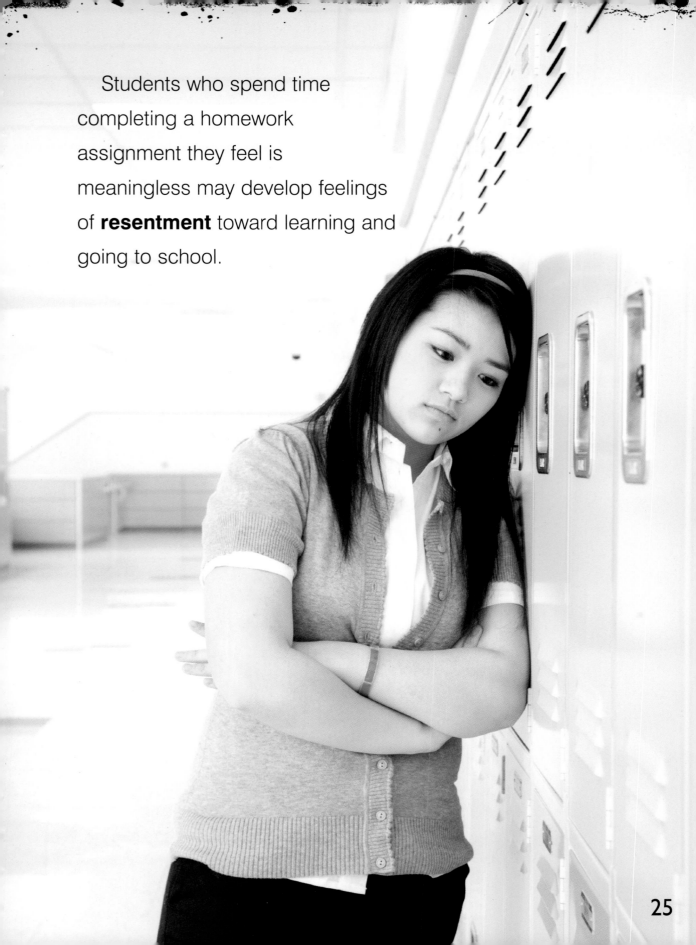

Students who spend time completing a homework assignment they feel is meaningless may develop feelings of **resentment** toward learning and going to school.

Proponents of homework say it makes students better learners and helps them perform better on tests.

Homework should not be given to every student unless it will benefit everyone in the class equally. It should provide value to the student and help them succeed.

A National School Board Association's Center for Public Education report says that there is no conclusive proof that homework increases students' success.

Your Turn

So what do you think about homework now that you've seen the issue from both sides? Each side's argument included facts, research, and examples. Which side do you think had the strongest points? What arguments would you add or expand on?

Think about your **position** on this issue. You may agree with some of the other side's argument. You may disagree with some of the reasons given by the side you support. Write your own opinion paper that includes facts, details, and examples. You may want to include stories from your own experiences as a student.

Telling Your Side: Writing Opinion Pieces

- Tell your opinion first. Use phrases such as:
  - *I like _____.*
  - *I think_____.*
  - *_____ is the best _____.*
- Give multiple reasons to support your opinion. Use facts and relevant information instead of stating your feelings.
- Use the words *and*, *because*, and *also* to connect your opinion to your reasons.
- Clarify or explain your facts by using the phrases *for example* or *such as*.
- Compare your opinion to a different opinion. Then point out reasons that your opinion is better. You can use phrases such as:
- *Some people think_____, but I disagree because _____.*
- *_____ is better than _____ because _____.*
- Give examples of positive outcomes if the reader agrees with your opinion. For example, you can use the phrase,
  If _____ then _____.
- Use a personal story about your own experiences with your topic. For example, if you are writing about your opinion on after-school sports, you can write about your own experiences with after-school sports activities.
- Finish your opinion piece with a strong conclusion that highlights your strongest arguments. Restate your opinion so your reader remembers how you feel.

Glossary

allotted (uh- LAHT-ed): set aside for a particular purpose

complex (KAHM-pleks): complicated

effective (i-FEK-tiv): skillful and able to get things done

element (EL-uh-muhnt): one of the simple, basic parts
of something

isolated (EYE-suh-lay-ted): alone or separate

mischief (MIS-chif): playful behavior that may cause
annoyance or harm to others

position (puh-ZISH-uhn): a person's opinion or point of view

proponents (pro-POH-nuhnts): people who advocate for or
support something

resentment (ri-ZENT-muhnt): anger or annoyance

sacrifice (SAK-ruh-fise): to give up something you value or
enjoy for the sake of something else

Index

Show What You Know

1. Both sides of the homework argument used data from scientific studies to support its position. How does this type of information make an argument stronger?

2. Why should you use personal examples to explain your opinion?

3. Why is it important to use facts and data in opinion pieces rather than just talking about the way a topic makes you feel?

4. Do you think it is easy to persuade people to change their opinion? Why or why not?

5. Is it possible to agree with points on both sides of an issue?

Websites to Visit

https://kids.usa.gov
www.discoveryeducation.com/students
http://mag.amazing-kids.org

About the Author

Reese Everett loves learning but isn't a big fan of homework. Unless it's awesome homework, then she loves it. (She is also not a fan of wearing socks unless they are awesome socks.) Reese writes books and articles about anything and everything for kids and adults. She has four kids who live with her in sunny Tampa, Florida.

Meet The Author!
www.meetREMauthors.com

www.rourkeeducationalmedia.com

PHOTO CREDITS: Cover: ©Tom Perkins; page 1: ©webstrana; page 3: ©Triggerphoto; page 4, 26: ©Susan Chiang; page 5: ©vadimguzhva; page 6: © Chris Ryan; page 6, 9, 11, 13, 15, 22: ©loops7; page 7, 24, : ©3bugsmom; page 8: ©David Sacks; page 9: ©littleny; page 10: ©Monkeybusinessimages; page 11: ©akatz; page 12: ©Yinyang; page 13: ©Constantine Pankin; page 15: ©Pino Bucca; page 16: ©ImageSource; page 17: ©Spotmatik Ltd; page 19: ©Heatherc333; page 20: ©Willie B. Thomas; page 21: ©comodigit; page 23: ©Mjth; page 25: ©Lifesizeimages; page 28: ©luminaimages; page 29: ©Sezeryadigar; page 30: ©evirgen

Edited by: Keli Sipperley

Cover design and Interior design by: Rhea Magaro

Library of Congress PCN Data

Homework, Yes or No / Reese Everett
 (Seeing Both Sides)
  ISBN 978-1-68191-380-3 (hard cover)
  ISBN 978-1-68191-422-0 (soft cover)
  ISBN 978-1-68191-462-6 (e-Book)
Library of Congress Control Number: 2015951543

Also Available as:

Printed in the United States of America, North Mankato, Minnesota